HOT TOPICS

WILD WEATHER

CHRYSALIS CHILDREN'S BOOKS

Useful internet websites

Check these out to find out more about weather and climate:

http://www.factmonster.com/science.html
Click on the Almanac 'Weather' section and scroll down to 'Natural Disasters' to discover
the havoc weather can wreak on our planet.

http://www.atozkidsstuff.com/weather.html
This site features simple weather experiments. Learn to measure rainfall or make frost at home!

http://school.discovery.com/sciencefaircentral/jakesattic/lab/acidrain/index.html
Find out what acid rain is and how it affects the environment.

http://www.snowcrystals.net
This site is all about snow crystals and snowflakes, and how these amazing structures are formed.

http://www.nhc.noaa.gov
This is the US national hurricane centre. You can view the latest satellite imagery and discover the
deadliest and most intense hurricanes. Learn what to do should you get caught in a hurricane!

http://www.hurricanehunters.com
Peruse the gallery of great hurricane photos and follow the hunters right into the eye of a storm.

http://www.ucar.edu/40th/webweather
Great facts about thunderstorms. Learn how to make lightning, a thunderstorm and a tornado!

http://www.brainpop.com/science/weather
Watch movies on anything from wind to temperature. Do experiments with Bob the rat.

http://kids.earth.nasa.gov/archive/nino
Learn all about El Niño and why it threatens the great coral reefs. Try out the science activities.

http://www.wildwildweather.com
Packed with facts, quizzes and games. Learn how meteorologists predict the weather.

http://www.bbc.co.uk/weather/weatherwise
Become a weather detective and beat the forecasters at their own game! Learn about
'crazy' weather and find out the 'secrets' of clouds.

http://www.epa.gov/globalwarming/kids
Click on 'Greenhouse Effect' and discover what is causing our planet to warm up.

Written by Harry Ford and Kay Barnham
Illustrated by Peter Bull, Arcana Studios,
Derek Fisher and Guy Smith
Cover designed by Clare Sleven

Editor: Rasha Elsaeed

This edition published in the UK in 2003 by
Chrysalis Children's Books PLC
64 Brewery Road, London N7 9NT

Every effort has been made to ensure none
of the recommended websites in this book is
linked to inappropriate material. However,
due to the ever-changing nature of the
Internet, the publishers regret they cannot take
responsibility for future content of these websites.

British Library Cataloguing in Publication Data
for this book is available from the British Library.

ISBN 1 904516 03 3

Printed and bound in China

Contents

Planet Mars also spins with a tilted axis so it has seasons very similar to Earth.  Mars

What is weather?

People who study the weather are called meteorologists. People who study climate are called climatologists.

Weather is the name given to the changing conditions of the atmosphere, or air, which surrounds the Earth. Weather conditions include wind, storms, rain, snow and sunshine.

Q What is climate?

A The average weather conditions over a long period of time - usually 10 to 30 years.

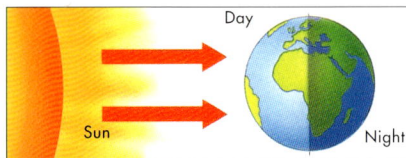

Day

Sun

Night

Q Why do we have day and night?

A During every 24 hours, the Earth spins around on its axis (an imaginary line joining the North Pole, the centre of the Earth and the South Pole), turning us towards the light of the Sun and away again, thus giving us night and day.

Q What is atmosphere?

A The mixture of gases that surround the Earth, made up of nitrogen, oxygen, water vapour and tiny amounts of other gases. Without these protective gases, human beings could not survive on the Earth. They protect us from the scorching rays of the Sun and from the icy chill of the night.

Stratopause   40 km

Ozone layer   15-30 km

Tropopause   12 km

aircraft

high cloud

The hottest place on Earth is Dallol in Ethiopia, where the average temperature is 34.4°C in the shade.

Q How is the atmosphere held around the Earth?

A The force of gravity pulls the gases of the atmosphere towards the Earth and prevents them from escaping into space.

Q Which are the hottest and coldest times of the day?

A The hottest time of the day is usually around 2 or 3 pm, while the coldest time is usually at sunrise.

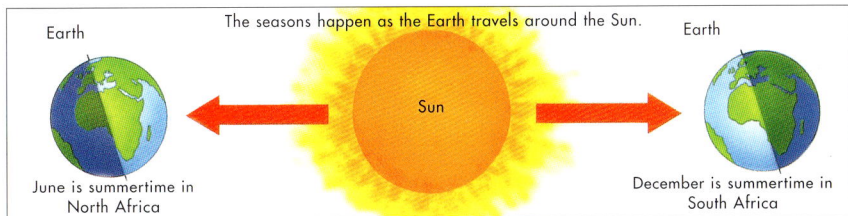

The seasons happen as the Earth travels around the Sun.

Earth

Earth

Sun

June is summertime in North Africa

December is summertime in South Africa

Q Why do we have seasons?

A The four seasons - spring, summer, autumn and winter - are caused by the tilt of the Earth's axis. As the Earth moves around on its axis, different parts are tilted towards the Sun for a few months at a time. The part leaning towards the Sun has summer, while the part leaning away has winter.

The weather happens in the lowest level of the atmosphere.

Q Where are the hottest and coldest places on Earth?

A The tropical regions, close to the Equator, the hottest because the Sun's rays are most concentrated there. The coldest places are the North Pole and the South Pole, where the Sun is so low in the sky that its power is spread over a vast area.

North Pole

Equator

South Pole

What is air pressure?

Although we cannot see it, air has weight which causes it to press down on the Earth and everything on it. Changes in the air pressure affect the weather.

Q Why is air pressure important to weather forecasters?

A Air pressure changes constantly, bringing different types of weather. These changes help weather forecasters to predict rainy weather, which usually comes with low pressure, and dry weather, which comes with high pressure.

Q Can we feel air pressure?

A No, not usually. However, occasionally when you go up or down a hill in a car, your ears may feel funny due to the change of air pressure. The same thing can happen in an aircraft.

Mountain top - 320 millibars

Q How do meteorologists measure the changes in air pressure?

A Pressure is measured with a barometer in units called millibars. Aneroid barometers contain hollow capsules with no air inside. As the pressure of the air alters, the capsules change shape and slowly move the pointer on the dial to show whether the air pressure is rising or falling.

An aneroid barometer

Q Why is air pressure lower at the top of mountains?

A Because there is less air pressing down from above. The lower air pressure makes the air thinner and harder to breathe.

High ground - 900 millibars

The cabins of aircraft are specially pressurised so that the crew and passengers do not suffer from less and less air pressure the higher the plane flies.

Q What is Buys Ballot's Law?

A The law for wind direction. The law states that when you stand with your back to the wind in the northern hemisphere you have high pressure on your right and low pressure on your left. In the southern hemisphere it is the reverse.

Low pressure

Q What is an isobar?

A Isobars are lines on weather maps that link places with the same air pressure. Weather people use these maps to forecast the weather for the next day.

Isobars are usually shown at intervals of 4 millibars.

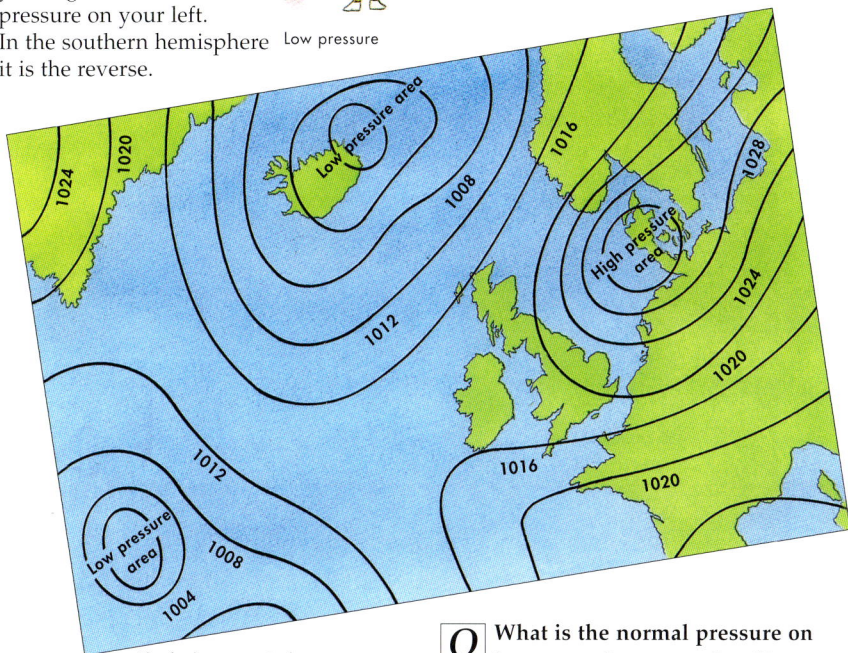

1024 1020 1008 1016 1028
Low pressure area
1012
High pressure area
1024
1020
1012 1016
Low pressure area 1008 1020
1004

The further apart isobars are, the lighter the wind.

Q What is the normal pressure on low ground, near sea level?

A Normal pressure at this low level is about 1,000 millibars.

Sea-level - 1,000 millibars

The world's windiest place is Commonwealth Bay, Antarctica.

What is wind?

A weather vane shows the wind direction.

Wind is air moving from one place to another as it warms up or cools down.

Q What makes the wind blow?

A The wind blows because cold air is continually moving in to replace rising warm air. As the Sun warms up different parts of the Earth's surface, the air above it is also warmed. Warm air becomes lighter and rises above surrounding cold air. In other places, the air cools, becomes heavier and sinks.

Q How is wind speed measured?

A An instrument called an anemometer measures wind speed. It has three or four metal cups at the end of arms which blow around slowly in a light breeze. The faster the wind blows, the faster the cups spin round.

An anemometer

Q What is the Beaufort Scale?

A This is a method of estimating the wind speed if you don't have an anemometer.

Force 1 - smoke drifts slowly

Force 2 - leaves rustle

Force 3 - leaves and small twigs move

Force 4 - small branches move

Force 5 - small trees with leaves sway

Force 6 - large branches move

Force 7 - whole trees sway

Gale force 8 - twigs break off trees, and walking is difficult

Q What is a tornado?

A This is a small whirling spiral of strong wind. Although much smaller than a hurricane, it is very powerful and can toss people, cars and even buildings into the air There is more about tornadoes on page 19.

Powerful tornadoes are common in central U.S.A.,especially in the area known as 'tornado alley' through Kansas and Oklahoma.

Q What is the difference between a gust of wind and a lull?

A A gust is an abrupt rush of wind. A lull is when the wind gets lighter for a few seconds.

Q What is a hurricane?

A This is a violent storm that starts when warm, wet air over the sea rises and forms huge columns of cloud full of water vapour. More air rushes in below the rising warm air and begins to spiral around at up to 300 km per hour. These fierce winds cause massive waves at sea and sometimes on the coast. When they 'hit' the land they often cause enormous destruction.

A typical Mediterranean windmill.

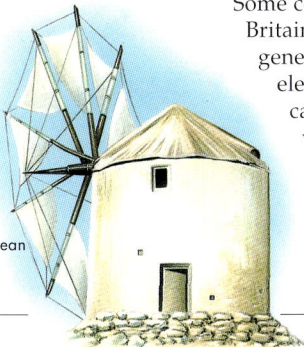

Q How can people use the wind?

A Wind power can be used in various ways. In flat countries people still use windmills to grind corn and pump water. Some countries, such as Britain, build wind generators to generate electricity. The wind can also be used for windsurfing, sailing and for flying kites.

A modern wind generator.

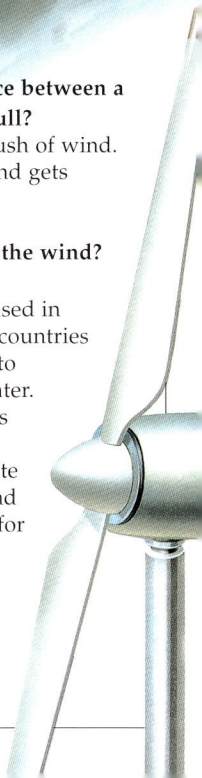

When air is forced upwards over a barrier such as hills or mountains, clouds form.

What are clouds?

Clouds are made up of billions of tiny drops of water. They form in different shapes and at different heights in the sky.

Q How does a cloud form?

A A cloud forms when moist air rises upwards. As the air cools, it expands and changes, or condenses, into tiny water droplets. The highest clouds contain ice crystals.

Warm air rises   It condenses   A cloud forms

Q Can aircraft fly through clouds?

A Yes, very easily. The water drops, or ice crystals, are so tiny that they barely affect an aircraft's progress. Usually an aircraft will climb through the clouds into the sunshine above.

Q Why do scientists study clouds?

A Scientists in weather stations around the world make daily observations of cloud formations. The results help them forecast the kind of weather to come.

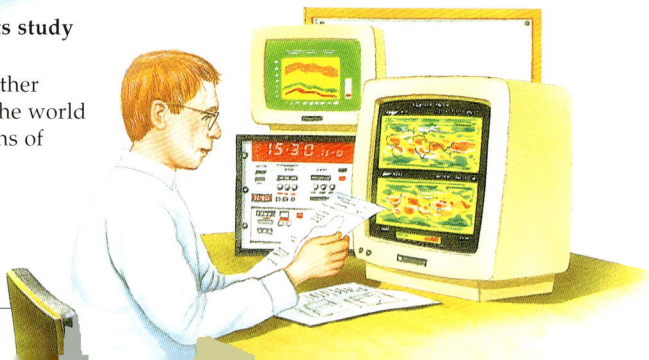

Aircraft sometimes leave artificial cloud trails behind them called contrails. They are made of ice crystals.

Q What are the highest clouds?

A There are there types of high clouds: *cirrus* clouds from in thin wispy streaks; *cirrostratus* clouds make a pale, high layer; and *cirrocumulus* are tiny lumps of cloud that look like beads or pearls.

Cirrus

Cirrostratus

Cirrocumulus

Altocumulus

Q What clouds form the middle cloud layer?

A There are three types: *altocumulus* clouds that form a higher, lumpy layer; *altostratus* clouds, making a pale, white layer; and *nimbostratus* clouds - a grey layer which produces rain or snow.

Nimbostratus

Altostratus

Cumulonimbus

Q What are the lowest clouds?

A There are four types of low clouds. Stratus clouds form a low, grey layer that often covers the tops of hills; *stratocumulus* clouds make an uneven, patchy layer; *cumulus* clouds - sometimes called 'cotton-wool' clouds; and *cumulonimbus* clouds - the dark storm clouds.

Cumulus

Stratocumulus

Stratus

The driest place in the world is the Atacama desert in Chile, where the rainfall is less than 0.1 millimetre per year.

Why do we need rain?

Rain provides the water that is necessary for the survival of plants, animals and humans. Without rain almost the only life on Earth would be in the oceans.

Q What makes it rain?

A As the Sun heats up Earth's oceans and rivers, water turns into an invisible gas called water vapour. As the vapour rises it turns into water droplets, which eventually form a cloud. The droplets continue growing until they are so heavy that they fall to the ground as rain. In this way, the same water evaporates and turns into rain again and again. This is known as the water cycle.

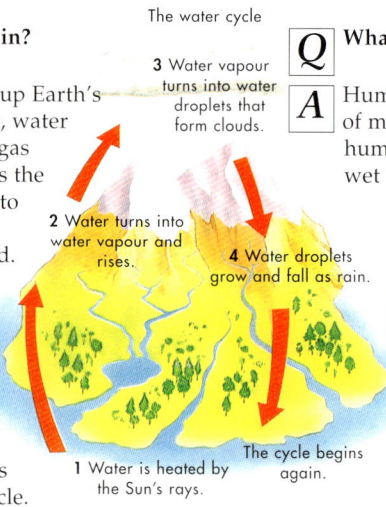

The water cycle

3 Water vapour turns into water droplets that form clouds.

2 Water turns into water vapour and rises.

4 Water droplets grow and fall as rain.

1 Water is heated by the Sun's rays.

The cycle begins again.

Q What is humidity?

A Humidity is the amount of moisture in the air. Very humid air can be a sign of wet weather to come.

Q How is rainfall measured?

A Each day, rain collects in a rain gauge. This is often a simple metal container which catches the rain in a funnel at the top.

Q Does the amount of rainfall have much effect on the environment?

A Yes. In areas where the rainfall is heavy, such as the rain forests around the Equator, there are many different kinds of plants and animals. However, in deserts where the rainfall is less than 25 cm per year - there is very little plant or animal life.

Many deserts have no rain for years.

In rainforests, it rains nearly every day.

Mawsynram

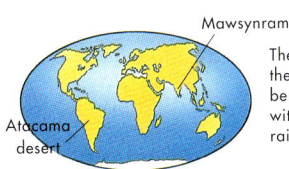

The wettest place in the world is thought to be Mawsynrarm, India, with 11,873 mm of rain per year.

Atacama desert

Q What causes floods?

A In hot countries floods are usually caused by thunderstorms. In cooler climates, low pressure areas may bring rain several times in a week until the rivers overflow their banks. Sometimes melting snow causes floods.

Severe drought makes soil dry out and crops fail. This can lead to the death of animals and people.

Q What is a monsoon?

A Monsoons bring heavy rains to India, Bangladesh and other parts of Asia every summer. The word 'monsoon' actually means a steady wind. However, because these summer-time winds bring heavy rains, the 'monsoon' is often used to describe the rains rather than the wind. In India, the torrential rains that the monsoon brings - known as the 'rainy season' - are vital to farmers because most of the annual rainfall falls during them.

Q What is a drought?

A A drought is when a lack of rain over a long period causes a water shortage. For many years, the Sahel region of Africa suffered an almost continual drought. The people there were unable to grow crops or feed their animals, and thousands of people and animals died.

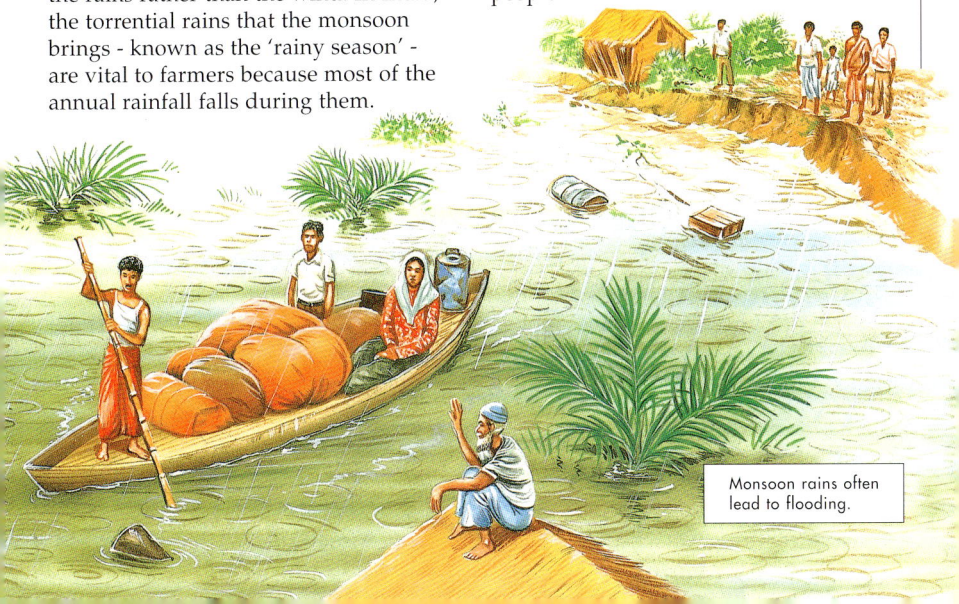

Monsoon rains often lead to flooding.

Some animals, such as polar bears, are specially adapted to live in a snowy climate.

When does it snow?

Polar bear

The heaviest snowfalls tend to occur when the temperature is around freezing point.

Q What makes it snow?

A When it is very cold the water in clouds freezes and forms snow crystals. As these crystals fall through the clouds they join with others and become snowflakes.

Q When is snow a nuisance or a danger?

A In heavy winds, snow can be blown into huge piles called snowdrifts. Snowdrifts block roads, and have to be cleared by big tractors with snowploughs on the front. In rural areas, snowdrifts can cut off whole villages, and supplies have to be dropped by helicopters. Snow can also bring down power lines, cutting off people's electricity.

Q When does the coldest weather occur?

A In most countries the coldest times are clear, calm nights when there are no clouds to keep the heat near the Earth's surface.

Q Can snow be useful?

A Yes. It can help crops - such as winter wheat - by protecting them from very hard frosts and cold dry winds. Also, it can be fun for skiing, sledging and for making snowballs and snowmen. In the past, the Inuit people of northern Canada and Greenland built houses, called 'igloos', out of snow.

All snowflakes have six sides, but no two are ever the same.

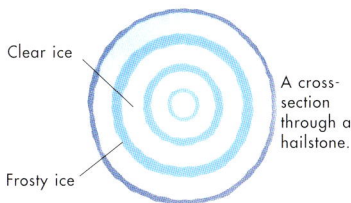

Clear ice

A cross-section through a hailstone.

Frosty ice

Hailstones are frozen raindrops that form in cumulonimbus clouds. As they fall through the clouds they melt then freeze, making frosty and icy layers.

Q What is the difference between snow and hail?

A Snowflakes are much lighter than hailstones, and have more air trapped inside. Hailstones are hard and heavy, like icy pellets. Hail comes out of cumulonimbus clouds, and can even fall in summer.

In very cold weather beautiful frost patterns can form on windows. Some people call this fern-like pattern 'Jack Frost's Garden'.

Q What is a frost?

A A frost is a temperature below freezing point. During a frost, ice crystals form on the grass or on the ground. Sometimes it looks so white that it could be mistaken for snow.

Q Can it snow during a thunderstorm?

A Yes, but this is quite rare. It might happen during the winter, particularly on the coast.

Q What is a blizzard?

A A blizzard is a snowstorm. Loose, powdery snow is whipped up by strong winds, sometimes making it impossible to see anything.

What colour is the sky?

Daylight comes from the Sun and is made up of the seven colours of the rainbow. As the Sun shines through clouds and reflects off raindrops, it produces combinations of these colours.

Q Why is the sky usually blue?

A Clear skies look blue because the atmosphere reflects mainly blue light from the Sun - this process is known as 'the scattering of light'. Towards sunset the sky looks red because the Sun's rays have to travel so far through the lower atmosphere that all the other colours are 'lost', or absorbed, and only red remains.

Q Does a red sunset mean that good weather will follow?

A Not necessarily. The old saying, 'Red sky at night, shepherd's delight', is not very reliable.

Q How are rainbows formed?

A By the sunlight reflecting off millions of raindrops. Each raindrop acts like a complicated mirror, splitting the Sun's rays into different beams of colour. The colours always appear in the same order - red, orange, yellow, green, blue, indigo and violet.

Q When can you see a rainbow?

A During, or after, a sudden shower on a sunny day. You must have your back to the Sun to see a rainbow.

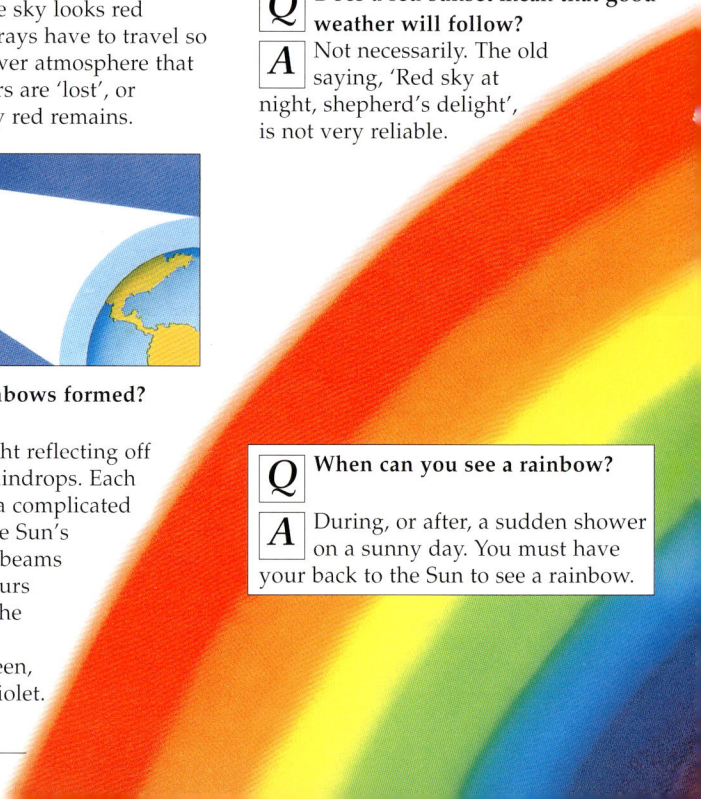

For 180 days a year, the North Pole and South Pole get no sunshine at all.

North Pole

South Pole

Q **Why does it sometimes get very dark during the day?**

A This happens when a very deep, thick cloud is reflecting most of the light from the Sun. All the water drops and ice crystals prevent the Sun's light from getting to the ground.

Q **When can you see the 'Northern Lights'?**

A Occasionally, on a clear night the sky above the Poles is lit up by a spectacular display of coloured lights known as Aurora Borealis, or 'Northern Lights'. The Aurora Australis, or 'Southern Lights', occurs near the Antarctic. These displays are caused by particles from the Sun reaching the very high part of the atmosphere.

Q **What causes a large 'halo' around the Sun?**

A This happens when the Sun shines through a thin, high layer of cirrostratus cloud made up of ice crystals. A smaller ring around the Sun, or Moon, called a 'corona' is formed by water droplets.

Benjamin Franklin's experiment with a kite linked to a metal key showed what lightning was made of when the key gave off sparks of electricity.

What causes thunderstorms?

When humid air rises quickly, cumulonimbus clouds form. Scientists think that ice crystals in the clouds rub together, creating electricity that is released as a flash of lightning. The lightning heats the air, causing the air to expand rapidly and create the noise of thunder.

Q Can you get thunder without, lightning?

A No, the two things always go together. Sometimes you might hear the thunder when you have missed seeing the lighting. At night you may see lightning but be too far away to hear the thunder.

Q What should you do if you are caught in a thunderstorm?

A Lightning tends to strike high things, such as tall trees and buildings, so if you are caught in a thunderstorm out in the open, crouch down on the ground or run for the shelter of a car or building. Do not take shelter under trees - this could be very dangerous!

Q What is sheet lightning?

A This is when the lightning is hidden by cloud but you can still see the brightness of the flash.

Q What is forked lightning?

A This is when lightning is not hidden behind cloud, and you can see the streak of lightning between cloud and ground. The streak is sometimes split into two or three branches. There is actually no difference between the sheet and fork lightning other than the way you see it.

The places with most thunderstorms a year are near the Equator. Bogor in Java has more than 220 thunderstorms. The least thundery places are in the Arctic and Antarctic.

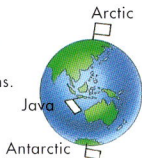

Q How can you measure the distance of a thunderstorm?

A When you see lightning, start counting the seconds until you hear the thunder. Divide the number of seconds by five to get the distance away in miles. To get the distance in kilometres, divide the number of seconds by three. This delay between thunder and lightning occurs because light travels much faster than sound.

Q What is St Elmo's Fire?

A This is static electricity which sometimes makes the masts of ships glow with light during thunderstorms.

Q Do tornadoes and thunderstorms ever occur together?

A Yes, sometimes. They both come with cumulonimbus clouds, though a tornado will only form with a very powerful cumulonimbus.

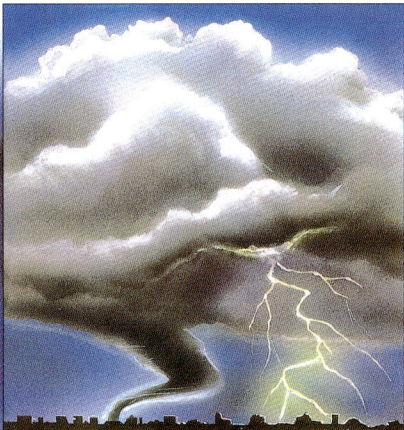

Q Can people be struck by lightning and survive?

A Yes. An American, Roy Sullivan, has been struck by lightning seven times and survived. However, occasionally cattle, sheep and even people are killed.

When the air is very clean visibility can be 160 km or more.

How is fog formed?

Fog occurs when water vapour near to the ground cools enough to turn into water droplets. You can sometimes see a similar thing happening to your breath on a cold morning.

Q Is fog the same as mist?

A Yes, mist and fog are basically the same thing. The only difference is that fog is thicker.

Q When is fog most likely to occur?

A Fog is most likely to occur when the skies are cloudless, the air is damp and the winds are light. Inland it usually occurs at night and sometimes lasts into morning. Sea fog can last through night and day.

A foggy morning can look very gloomy, but the fog may only be 200 metres deep. Above, the Sun could be shining.

Q What is acid rain?

A All rain is slightly acid. However acid rain falls when gases and chemicals from factories and car exhausts make the moisture in the air more acid. Acid rain kills trees, pollutes lakes and damages crops. Acid particles from the air can destroy buildings by eating away at the stonework even when it is not raining.

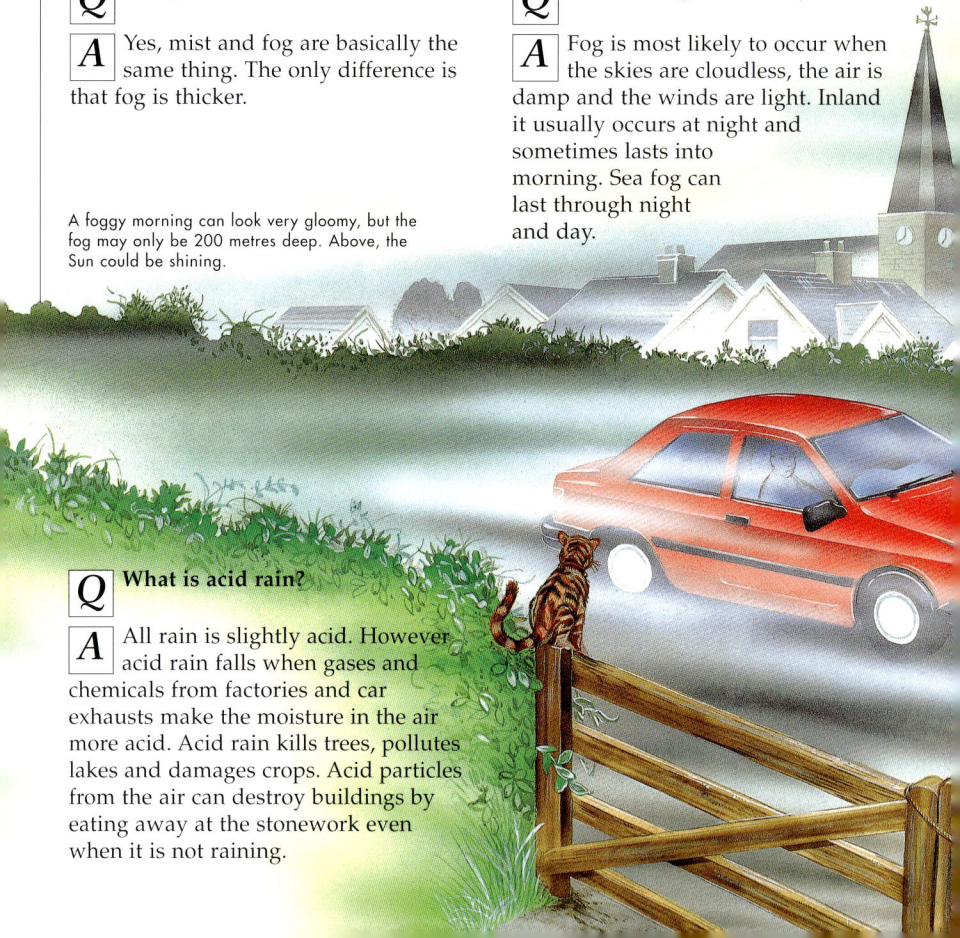

In Chile's dry Atacama desert, people use harps strung with nylon thread to collect water from sea fog.

Q What is smog?

A Smog is a combination of fog and smoke that occurs over cities and industrial areas. The main cause of this is the tiny particles from car-exhaust fumes and factory chimneys. Smog can last for several days and is particularly harmful to people with asthma and other breathing difficulties.

Q What effect does fog have on travel?

A Fog reduces visibility, which can cause accidents. Cars are slowed down, and train drivers have to reduce speed to see signals. Aircraft may not be able to take off, and those trying to land may have to divert to another airport where there is no fog.

Q Other than fog, what can make the atmosphere look hazy?

A Almost any solid particle can affect the atmosphere. This includes car-exhaust fumes, smoke from factories, desert dust and volcanic dust.

Q What effect do volcanoes have on the air?

A Close to the eruption there may be falling ash or dust, and perhaps a smell of sulphur. More dramatically, very fine dust floats into the sky and can give redder sunsets than usual for up to a year. Very occasionally, the Moon will look blue after an eruption because of the dust in the atmosphere.

In 1883, the volcanic island of Krakatoa erupted. The sunsets were redder for two years afterwards.

A strong gale at sea can create waves over 15 metres high. Some waves are caused by winds occurring 3,000 km away.

Is weather different at sea?

The most important difference between sea and land is the temperature. It is normally cooler at sea than inland during the day, but warmer at night.

Q Is the wind stronger over the sea?

A Yes, because the open sea has no hills, trees or buildings to slow down its speed.

Q What is a sea breeze?

A This is a wind that blows from the sea on to the coast on a warm, sunny day. It happens because the air over the land is heated up more quickly than the air over the sea. The warm air over the land rises and a current of cooler air moves in from the sea to replace it.

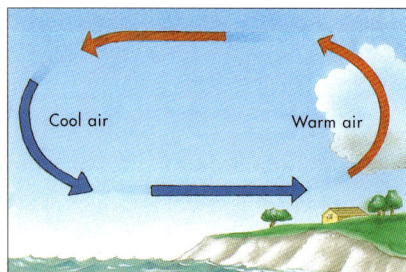

Q Is humidity different near the sea?

A Humidity is higher near the sea because water evaporates into the air. Evaporation is when water is warmed up and turned into water vapour. This is why puddles dry up on a sunny day.

On a sunny day, water evaporates, or dries up.

Q Do you get fog or thunder at sea?

A Yes, these can both occur. Fog is quite common in areas of cold sea, while thunder is common in hot regions, such as the Caribbean and Central Pacific.

Gales, fogs and storms can make conditions dangerous for sailors at sea.

Cool air

Warm air

Grand Banks, near Newfoundland, Canada, is the world's foggiest area of sea.

Q Is the weather better in coastal places than inland?

A It varies. Areas around the coast tend to be wetter and foggier than inland. Sea breezes also mean that summers are generally cooler. However, there is much less frost in coastal areas, and winters are normally milder.

Q Do oceans have much effect on Earth's climate?

A Yes, they absorb the Sun's heat and spread it around the world in currents. These currents are huge wind-driven rivers in the sea that heat or cool the air above them, creating hotter or cooler weather.

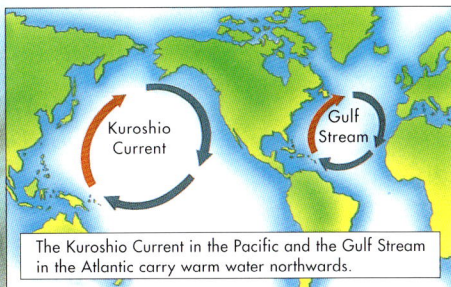

Kuroshio Current

Gulf Stream

The Kuroshio Current in the Pacific and the Gulf Stream in the Atlantic carry warm water northwards.

Q What weather conditions can be dangerous to sailors?

A Fog can drastically reduce visibility at sea. However, lighthouses, sirens, foghorns and radars all help ships to find their way in dense fogs. Gales can be more of a problem, whipping up waves and causing ships to slow down or even capsize.

In Canada's Rocky Mountains, warm winds blow that can raise the temperature by 20°C.

How strange can weather be?

All parts of the world occasionally get bizarre weather conditions. There have even been reports of red rain and summer snow.

Q Are there any cases of unusual snowfall?

A Yes. In 1975, snow in England prevented a summer cricket match, while in September 1981 snow fell in the Kalahari Desert, Africa, for the first time in living memory.

Q What causes coloured snow and rain to fall on the Alps?

A Red, pink and brown rain or snow sometimes falls over the Alps. This is caused by the coloured dust of the Sahara Desert being swept over 2,000 km by the wind.

Q What is a waterspout?

A A waterspout is simply a tornado that forms at sea. It is a swirling column of air that sucks up seawater and other things in its path. Although waterspouts are not as powerful as the tornadoes that form over land, they can still be very dangerous, especially to small boats. In the past, sailors used to think that distant waterspouts were sea monsters rising up from the waves!

Q Do unidentifiable substances ever fall from the sky?

A Yes, over the years there have been numerous reports of slimy material falling out of the sky. In 1978, a green slime fell on Washington, coating cars and buildings, killing plants and making animals sick. It has been suggested that the slime was caused by pesticide and jet exhaust fumes, but this has not been proven. Some people believe that these slimy materials could come from some sort of alien life form!

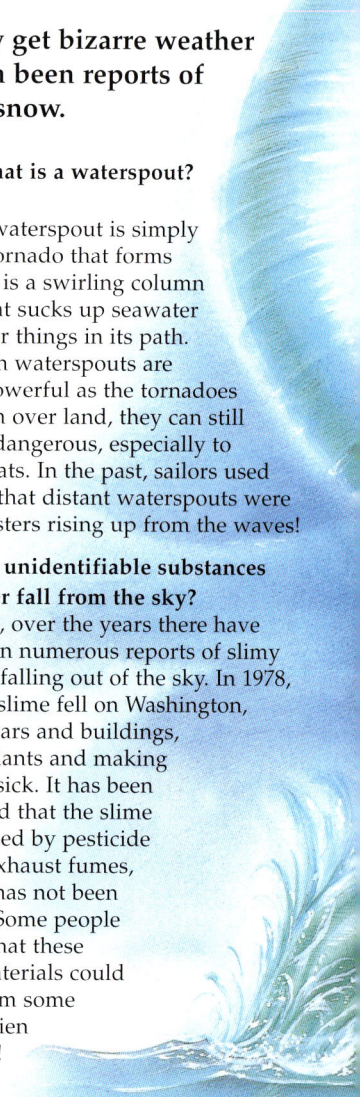

Q What is El Niño?

A This is a sudden warming every few years of the Pacific Ocean off the coast of South America. It spreads westwards and affects the weather of many countries. It is not yet fully understood.

Equator

El Niño

SOUTH AMERICA

PACIFIC OCEAN

Waterspouts are tornadoes that happen at sea.

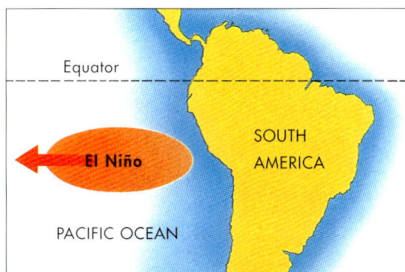

Q What is the world's record rainburst?

A In 1970, 38.1 mm of rain fell on Guadeloupe, in the West Indies, in just 90 seconds.

Q Can it really 'rain cats and dogs'?

A There don't appear to be any reports of it actually raining cats and dogs. However, there are reliable records from around the world of showers of fish, frogs, spiders, crabs and other creatures. Apparently, on 16 June 1939 a shower of tiny frogs fell on Trowbridge in England. It would seem that strong winds and waterspouts can suck up a whole variety of things and drop them some distance away.

How are forecasts made?

Nowadays, weather information from around the world is plotted on a synoptic chart and then fed into a computer. The computer works out what the next day's weather might be.

Q **How is weather information collected?**

A There are over 10,000 weather stations around the world. Many are in major cities and airports, while others are on weather ships. People working there make regular checks on visibility, wind speed and direction, humidity, air pressure and rainfall. In other places, balloons are launched to collect upper air information about jet streams and cold air above. Satellites also circle the Earth, sending down cloud and temperature patterns. Radars pick up signs of coming rain and storms.

Weather balloon

Satellite

Radar

Weather ship

Q **Is it easier to make a short-range forecast?**

A Yes. A radar display will show us where it is raining now and can compute where the rain will be in the next two hours.

Radar weather picture

Q **How accurate are weather forecasts?**

A Although weather forecasts try to be as accurate as possible, they are not always correct. Weather forecasters claim to be right eight out of ten times.

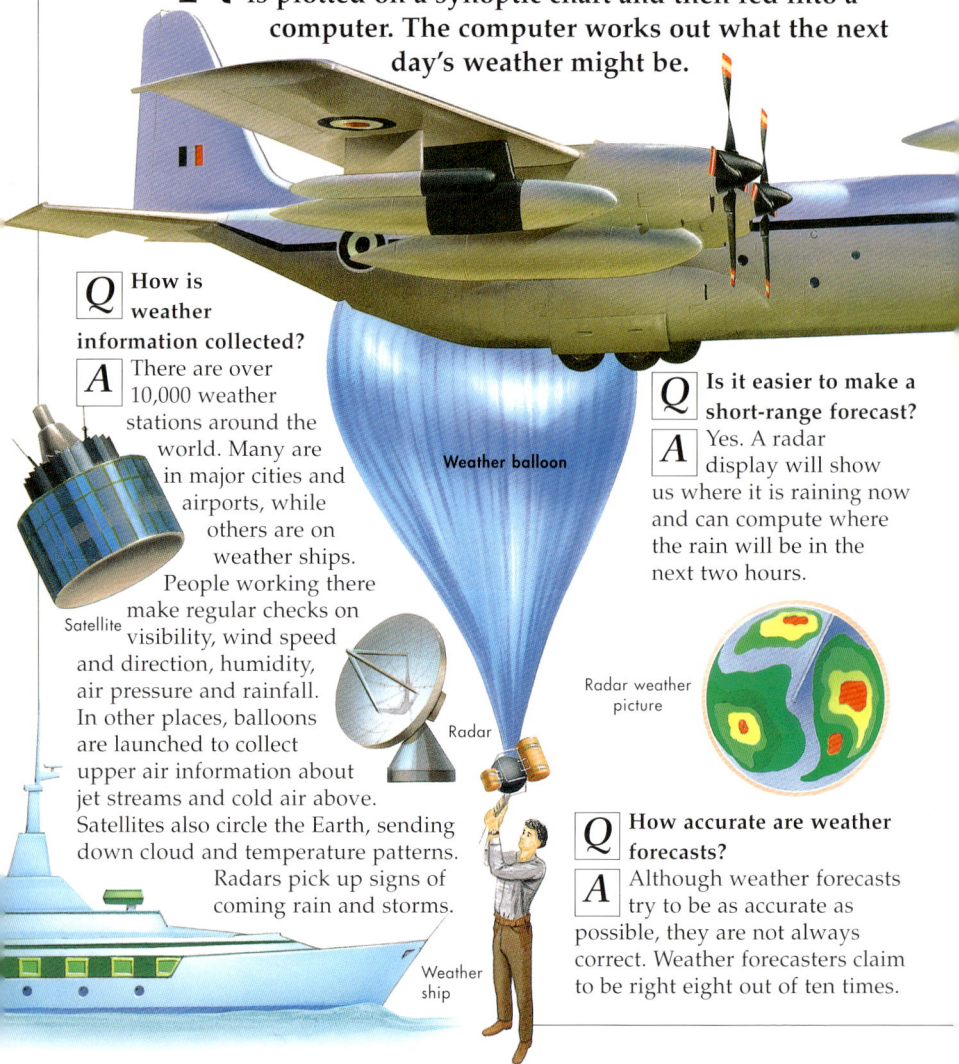

The word 'forecast' was first used to describe weather prediction in 1850 by Britain's then Chief Meteorologist, Admiral Fitzroy.

Q How far ahead can forecasts predict the weather?

A They can predict about one week ahead. Past weather records are sometimes used to forecast weather further ahead, but this is very unreliable.

Q Are all television weather people real meteorologists?

A No, not all. Some are professional presenters who work from a script provided by a weather centre. Others are scientists who do their own forecasts.

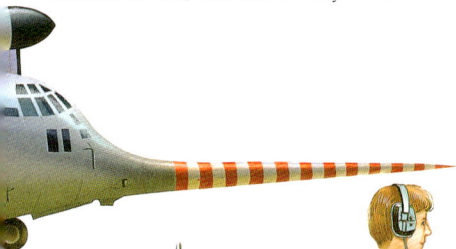

A weather station

Q Are there weather forecasts other than on television?

A Yes, lots of them. Forecasts are made for shipping, for aircraft, for road and rail travel and even for large shops. There are also forecasts in newspapers and on the radio.

Q How do you become a weather expert?

A At school you would need to study maths and physics. At university you could study meteorology. Degrees in maths, physics or oceanography can also lead to a career in meteorology.

A halo around the Sun can be the sign of an approaching warm front. Rain may follow within 12 hours.

Can we predict the weather?

Although the most accurate predictions come from meteorologists, anyone can make local weather predictions by watching the sky and using simple equipment.

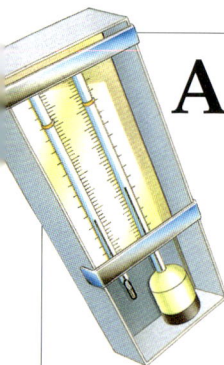

Q What equipment is it useful to have?

A A weather vane (look on a nearby church), a thermometer, a barometer and a rain gauge.

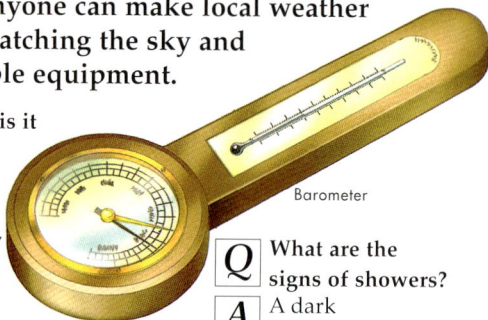

Thermometer

Barometer

Q How can you measure wind?

A You can measure wind direction with a weather vane, and wind speed with the Beaufort scale (see page 8). Remember that wind direction is the direction that the wind is blowing from.

Q What are the signs of showers?

A A dark cumulonimbus cloud may appear in the sky, especially on a spring or summer afternoon. Watch it carefully - if it's coming towards you, showers are probably on the way.

Dark cumulonimbus clouds are a sign of rain.

Weather vane

Q What are the signs of heavy, continuous rain on the way?

A A barometer will show a drop in air pressure and the sky will cloud over. High clouds, such as cirrostratus, will be replaced by thicker medium or low clouds.

Pine cones are said to be good weather forecasters. In dry weather, their scales open. if the cone is closed, it means rain is on the way.

Some people still believe that cows lie down when it is going to rain. However, scientists have studied many herds of cows and found that it is not true.

Q How can you measure rainfall?

A With a simple home-made rain gauge. Stand a large dish or bucket in the middle of an open space, such as a lawn. Each day tip the rainwater in a measuring jug to measure the amount.

Q Is country weather lore ever reliable?

A For centuries country people have looked to the world around them for signs of the coming weather. Although a lot of so-called 'country weather lore' is unreliable, some things in nature can give fairly accurate predictions. Seaweed is often used by natural weather forecasters. In dry weather it dries out and shrivels. If rain threatens it swells and feels damp to the touch.

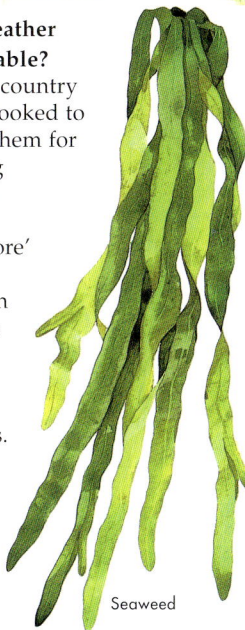

Seaweed

Q What should you do with all your observations?

A Keep a record of all your observations in a weather diary. Make a note of cloud amount, wind direction and wind speed, and any rain or snow. If you have a barometer and thermometer, write down the pressure and temperature at the same time each day. You could also record the 'state of the ground' - whether your lawn or backyard is wet, damp, dry, frosty or snowy.

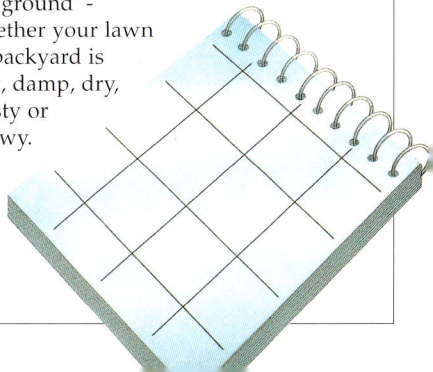

Exhaust fumes in our cities are one of the biggest problems. Electric cars and trains could be one solution.

Is our climate changing?

Scientists have estimated that by 2050, the Earth's temperature could have risen 2-4°C.

The world's climate is slowly changing, but we don't fully understand why. Thermometer readings show that, on average, it has got more than half a degree Celsius warmer in the last 100 years.

Q Is today's climate very different to that of fifty thousand years ago?

A Yes. Fifty thousand years ago the Earth was in the middle of the last ice age, and much of the Earth's surface was covered in a thick sheet of ice. This ice age came to an end about 15,000 years ago when the climate started to get warmer and the ice melted. The age we now live in is called 'interglacial'.

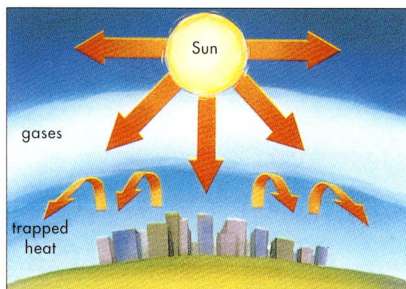

Q Is the greenhouse effect a good thing?

A No. If the greenhouse effect continues, some countries will become too hot. Also, less rain will fall in some areas, and crops won't grow. Some scientists believe that if the Earth becomes warmer, the Antarctic sheet will start to melt, flooding some low-lying areas.

Sun

gases

trapped heat

Q What is the greenhouse effect?

A The greenhouse effect is caused by cars, factories and power stations releasing gases, particularly carbon dioxide, into the atmosphere. Like a greenhouse, these gases trap heat and gradually make the climate warmer.

Pollution is slowly damaging our planet.

Many people believe that unless humans stop polluting the Earth with CFCs and carbon dioxide we could endanger all life on our planet.

Q What is the ozone layer?

A The ozone is a layer of gas very high in the atmosphere. This layer protects us from the Sun's harmful ultraviolet rays.

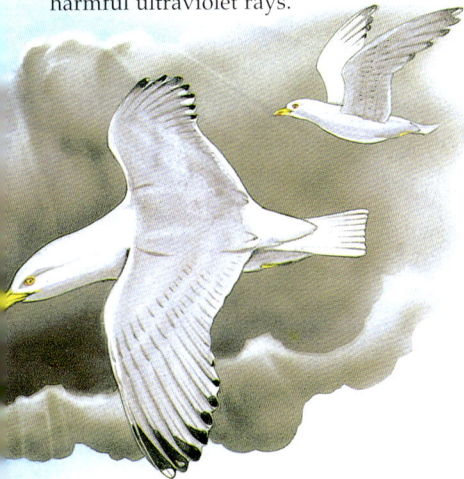

Q Is there a hole in the ozone layer?

A Although the ozone layer has become thin in many places, there are no actual holes in it. However, it is being destroyed by chemicals called chlorofluorocarbons (CFCs), which are used in aerosol sprays and in fridges.

A satellite picture of Earth showing the thinning zone layer.

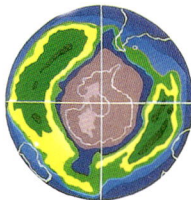

Q How can the destruction of the rain forests affect the weather?

A The world's rain forests are being cut down or burnt at a rate of around 24 square km per hour. If this continues it could lead to dramatic changes in rainfall and temperature patterns.

Q Can we stop some of these climate changes?

A Yes, but it will need a big effort by everyone, especially in rich countries. You could do your part by conserving power and cutting down on ways you pollute the Earth. Switch lights off when you leave a room and put on an extra jumper rather than turn up the heating. Avoid using things that contain CFCs and walk or cycle for short journeys rather than travel in a car.

Index

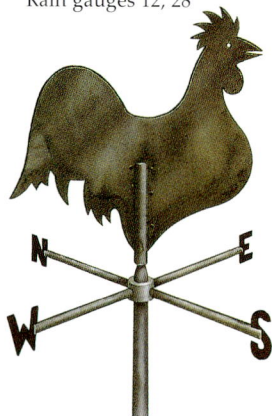